THE ATHENIAN ACROPOLIS

Editor: Costas Adam
Texts: Maria Brouscari
Translation: Alexandra Doumas
Photographs: Yannis Yannelos
Printing: Pergamos S.A.

MARIA S. BROUSCARI

THE ATHENIAN ACROPOLIS

ΕΚΔΟΣΕΙΣ
ADAM
EDITIONS

The Acropolis from the west.

HISTORICAL BACKGROUND

In prehistoric times, long before the Acropolis, one of the hills rising from the plain of Attica, became the most revered and sacred official sanctuary of Athens, it was the site of a settlement and the residence of the local ruler.

Though neither the highest nor the most extensive hill in the area, it has distinct advantages over those nearby, which is why man chose to live there even in Neolithic times. Its fairly level surface is sufficiently wide to accommodate the installation of several people. All its slopes are precipitous - and thus ensured its protection - excepting one, the west, which is a more gentle approach and relatively easy to guard. There are also springs of potable water, a basic prerequisite for effective resistance in the event of siege. The Acropolis was the seat of the overlord of the city, who lived in the *megaron* with his family, entourage and personal guard. The settlement proper developed around the citadel

Panoramic view of the Acropolis
with the Aegina and the Saronic
Gulf beyond.

hill, and actually comprised several loosely connected villages, which explains why for many centuries the name Athens was in fact used in the plural.

In those far-off times Athens was one of the many independent cities of Attica, some of which were very wealthy and possibly mightier, such as Marathon, Thorikos and others. As the centuries rolled by, however, the power and influence of the ruler of Athens steadily increased, perhaps because of the city's central location, and by the 14th century BC the *anax* (as he was known) - probably Theseus who figures in later myths - was able to impose his will on the other cities and unite them in a single state, with Athens *primus inter pares*. In the following century, under the threat of hostile incursions which had already begun to disrupt the old order in Greece, the *anax* fortified the hill of the Acropolis with a strong defensive wall of enormous, irregular boulders, just like the ramparts of contemporary citadels, such as at Mycenae, Tiryns and elsewhere. In later times the fortification wall of Athens was dubbed Cyclopean, for it was believed that only beings with supernatural strength, as the Cyclops were imagined to be, could have built such an enormous structure.

The *anax* was not only the political and military leader of his people, he had religious and ritual power too. The palace was the focus of the official cult of a goddess, protectress of vegetation, fruits, birth, man's fecundity and the city (Athena Polias). Her beloved plant was the olive. On the valuable evidence of the Linear B tablets from Knossos, which mention a female deity ATANA POTINIJA (Athena Potnia), it would seem that this goddess was already known as Athena, after whom the city of which she was patron was named. Thus, within the area of the palace, the subsequent sanctuary gradually came into being.

Around the year 1000 BC, or slightly later, the monarchy was eventually replaced by the aristocracy, that is political responsibility was shared between the aristocrats, noble landowners. The seat of government was transferred to the lower city, the *asty*, since the aristocrats feared the potential power that could be vested in a political authority installed in the citadel, and the Acropolis became solely a place of worship.The palace gradually fell into ruins and on its site a temple to the goddess Athena was erected. This was the "well-built domus of Erechtheus" (the name of a king of prehistoric Athens), the "rich temple" of Homer, in which the primitive wooden *hedos or xoanon of* Athena, which the Athenians believe had fallen from heaven *(diipetes),* was kept. The Athenians carried out magnificent sacrifices on the altar in front of the building and they revered certain other "sacred signs" in the vicinity, one of which was the olive tree believed to have been revealed by Athena during her quarrel with the sea god Poseidon for dominion over Attica. The cult of Poseidon, a Peloponnesian deity, had been brought to Athens by the Neleides, who fled from Pylos and sought refuge in the city to escape the Dorian invaders at the end of the prehistoric period. Tradition relates that in the course of his dispute with Athena, Poseidon had struck the rock with his trident, causing brackish water (symbolic of the sea) to gush forth. Indeed, centuries later, the Athenians pointed out the other "sacred sign" beside Athena's olive tree, the "sea", as well as the mark left by Poseidon's trident on the rock. As time passed the Athenians reconciled the two former rivals and both were worshipped under the same roof (see chapters on the "Archaios Naos" and the Erechtheum). From this somewhat primitive phase until the end of antiquity, there was a chamber dedicated to Poseidon in the temple of Athena, behind that of the goddess (see below). The temple was also home to a sacred snake, Erichthonios, guardian of the Acropolis, and in this same vicinity was the tomb of the mythical king of Athens, Cecrops.

Even in those early times the Athenians made offerings in the sanctuary of the Acropolis. These were usually tripods or statuettes of bronze, of the kind familiar from other Greek sanctuaries. Their wealth and variety bespeak not only the deep love the Athenians had for their goddess, but also their considerable prosperity.

At the beginning of the 6th century BC the small temple of Athena was replaced by a much larger one, to which the *xoanon* of the goddess was transferred. Thus the new temple continued to be the holiest of all the Athenian sanctuaries. Like its predecessor it too was known as the "Archaios Naos", which name it later bequeathed to the building raised in its stead in the 5th century BC (known in Roman times as the Erechtheum).

It seems that during the time of the tyrant Peisistratos, who was the adroit and able ruler of Athens for many years, from the middle of the 6th century BC onwards, a second large temple was erected, a few metres lower down, to the south; the first Parthenon. This too was dedicated to Athena, though not as the peace-loving "Polias", like the old one, but as the martial virgin "Pallas", the fully-armed patron-deity of the city whose power was just beginning to spread overseas. The era of Peisistratos' tyranny, and of his sons who succeeded him on his death in 527 BC until the assassination of one, Hipparchos (514 BC) and the overthrow of the other, Hippias (509 BC), was one of sustained political, economic, artistic and intellectual acme for Athens. The city became one of the leading centres of Hellenism and its goddess was the recipient of ever richer and choicer gifts. Marble statues, outstanding among which were those of young maidens clad in elaborately pleated, brightly coloured garments and with a distinctive enigmatic smile, the *korai,* as well as statuettes of bronze, painted vases of exceptional quality, and other *ex votos* of all kinds, filled the sanctuary. Small edifices, "Treasuries", were built between the large temples. The crest of this wave of artistic expression was maintained even after Cleisthenes installed the Democracy in 508 BC.

After their splendid victory at Marathon, the Athenians decided to express their gratitude to their patron-goddess in the most magnificent manner. They built a second great temple to Athena, next to the "Archaios Naos" (on the site now occupied by the Parthenon). This temple glorified the goddess's martial aspect (Pallas Athena), thanks to which they had vanquished the Medes.

In one fell swoop this rich, vivid and festive aspect of the Acropolis was swept away by the Persians, who invaded Greece and captured Athens in 480 BC. They set fire to the buildings, tore down the statues, smashed the vases and other votive offerings in a frenzy of destruction. When the Athenians returned to their city two years later, after their victories at Salamis and Plataea, they beheld a terrible sight; a heap of ruins and wreckage. However, they did not throw the débris out of the area of the Acropolis in order to start anew, but respectfully buried the fragments as holy heirlooms, on the spot, in special pits which they then covered over with earth. There they were to remain hidden for some two thousand years, thus escaping more recent and devastating catastrophes, until they were brought to light by the archaeologist's pick, from 1886 onwards.

With the victory at Salamis, and that at Plataea, but above all with the founding of the alliance of Greek cities of the Aegean, centred on the Sanctuary of Apollo on Delos but under the hegemony of Athens, the city rose to pre-eminence in the Hellenic world. Cimon, son of Miltiades, the victor at Marathon, built the south rampart of the Acropolis, known as the Cimoneian wall. Part of the "Archaios Naos" was repaired in order to house the venerable *xoanon* of the goddess, and also served as the treasury of the state. However, the sons of those who had defeated the Medes did not dare proceed with rebuilding the second large temple on the Acropolis or the other temples in the city. They respected the oath sworn by their fathers before the battle of Plataea, not to rebuild the temples destroyed by the Persians.

After Cimon's death and the dominance of the radical democratic faction, led by Pericles, himself a member of the great and old-established Alcmaeonid family, the situation changed. Pericles' vision of Athens was not only as political leader of the Greek world but also as its artistic centre. His desire was to fill the Acropolis, Athens, the whole of Attica, with monuments worthy of the illustrious past and of emulation by all Greeks. To this end he convened a pan-Hellenic assembly to discuss the restoration of the sanctuaries destroyed by the Persians, but his plans were thwarted by Sparta. Undaunted, he was thus free to go ahead on his own. The major obstacle, the economic one, was overcome, not only because the city's coffers were well-filled, but because, henceforth, part of the funds of the League, the treasury of which had been moved from Delos to Athens in 454 BC, were spent on the works. There was no shortage of artistic talent, for artists of all kinds already abounded in Athens and even more were attracted there from other cities, on account of its flourishing economy and international standing. Most important of all, Pericles was surrounded by a select circle of friends, among whom was the extraordinarily gifted sculptor and painter, Phidias. Pericles appointed him overseer‚of the project and also commissioned him to draw up the general plans of the artistic programme and supervise its execution. Pericles managed to win the support of the *demos* of Athens in this venture. The first and grandest of all his works was the Parthenon, designed by the architects Ictinos and Callicrates, the building of which commenced in 447 BC and finished in 438 BC (work continued on the pediments until 432 BC). In 438 BC work began on the Propylaea, the construction of which was interrupted in 432 BC, because of the Peloponnesian War. Once again the sanctuary (like Athens and Attica in general) was filled with a host of significant *ex votos,* the creations of great artists, outstanding among which were the enormous bronze statue of Athena Promachos, sculpted by Phidias, set up in the area between the Propylaea and the Parthenon *circa* 460 BC (before they were actually built). Pericles' grandiose project was brought to a halt before completion, on the outbreak of war, and its motive force died of the plague in 429 BC.

Nevertheless, the favourable turn of events after 425 BC, in particular the Nician peace (421 BC), enabled the Athenians to resume works on the Acropolis. Between 425 and 421 BC the little temple of Athena Nike was built, and in 421 BC work started on the construction of the Erechtheum. This stopped in 415 BC, when an expeditionary force was sent to Sicily, but begin again in 410 BC and the temple was completed just two years before the disastrous outcome of this war for Athens.

For several centuries after, only smallish edifices were built on the Acropolis, though the dedication of votive offerings, some of which were very valuable continued. In 27 BC a small, monopteral temple, dedicated to the goddess Roma and to Augustus, was erected in front of the entrance to the Parthenon.

The monuments of the Acropolis survived, more or less unscathed, the two major calamities which befell Athens . The first was the invasion by the Roman army under Sulla, in 86 BC, and the second that of the barbarian hordes of Herulae in AD 267. In the 1st century BC, part of the Erechtheum was badly damaged by fire, the cause of which is unknown, but it was repaired by the end of that century. The Parthenon was also affected by conflagration, though exactly when and what could have started it are not known.

An invaluable source of knowledge on the monuments and *ex votos* present on the Acropolis in the first centuries of the present era is the account given by the contemporary traveller (mid-2nd century AD) Pausanias, in his *Description of Greece.* Though his information is somewhat confused in places, this work is nevertheless fundamental to our understanding of those monuments and ruins still preserved today.

With the arrival of Christianity the fanatical converts to the new faith set about ridding the Acropolis of the votive offerings. Some were smashed, others stolen. The ivory and gold statue of Athena in the Parthenon and the bronze one of the Promachos, both sculpted by Phidias, were taken to Constantinople, where they were later destroyed, the first by fire and the second by the mob during the Crusaders' siege of the city in 1204. In the 6th century the Parthenon was transformed into a church of the Holy Wisdom (Aghia Sophia), but though certain changes were made (see below) it suffered little damage overall. It likewise remained unharmed when converted into a Catholic church after 1204.

Panoramic view of the Acropolis and Philopappus hill.

The Franks arranged the Propylaea as the palace of the Duke of Athens. The Erechtheum also became a church.

The Turks, who captured Athens in 1456, transformed the Parthenon into a mosque and erected a minaret at its southwest corner. The Propylaea served as the residence of the Turkish commander. His harem was installed in its west section.

In 1674 the French ambassador to Constantinople, the Marquis de Nointel, visited Athens and the Acropolis. He was granted a permit for an artist in his large entourage, Jacques Carrey, to make drawings of the Parthenon sculptures. Despite some misunderstanding of subjects, these drawings, executed just a few years before the destruction of the temple by Morosini, are a document of inestimable value. Two other European travellers, Spon and Wheler, also visited the Acropolis around this time.

In 1686, to meet the imminent threat of Athens' invasion by Venetian forces under Fr. Morosini, the Turks reinforced the fortifications of the Acropolis and constructed a mighty bastion on the approach to it, extending between the Nike tower and the Propylaea. This was constructed of building material from the Nike temple, which was demolished for this specific purpose.

The following year, as Morosini laid siege to the Acropolis, a shell from his artillery fell on the Parthenon, which the Turks were using as a gunpowder store. There was a tremendous explosion and a large part of the building was destroyed. Not only was serious damage caused to its structure, most of its sculpted decoration was irreparably destroyed too.

As visits by European travellers became more frequent in the 18th century, the monuments of the

Acropolis became increasingly well-known, thanks to their drawings and descriptions, attracting in-veterate collectors of antiquities like a magnet. The political weakness of the Ottoman state paved the way for the actual removal of works of art. At the beginning of the 19th century the British Ambas-sador to the Sublime Porte, Lord Elgin, taking advantage of the prevailing favourable pro-English clime, managed to obtain a permit from the Sultan to detach pieces and transport them to England. Assisted by the Neapolitan sculptor Lusieri, he removed the greater part of those Parthenon sculp-tures which had escaped the explosion, one of the *korai* from the Erechtheum (Caryatid), and a host of other works. Elgin's plundering of the Acropolis monuments, though by no means the only in-stance of theft of antiquities from Greece at that time, was on such a scale and included such impor-tant works of Classical art that it provoked an outcry even in England. One of his most vituperative opponents was the philhellene, Lord Byron. On his return to England, Elgin sold his collection to the British Museum and the so-called Elgin Marbles are still one of its most prized exhibits.

After the liberation of Athens from the Turks, work began on clearing the Acropolis of the ruins of the Turkish settlement there, which had been razed to the ground in the course of the fierce battles fought during the struggle for independence, particularly when Kiutahi besieged the Acropolis (1826-27). The Turkish bastion was dismantled and from its component material it was possible to reconsti-tute and restore the temple of Athena Nike between 1835 and 1840.

Restoration work was then begun on the Parthenon and the Erechtheum and some excavations were conducted on the surface of the rock, which yielded splendid and significant finds.

However, the most important excavations were those carried out between the years 1885 and 1890 by P. Kavvadias and the German Kawerau, who explored the greater part of the infill, right down to bedrock. The deposit included the so-called "Persian layer", a stratum created in 478 BC from the ruins of the buildings and *ex votos;* the result of the capture and destruction of the Acropolis by the Persians two years earlier.

Since the final years of the last century, systematic restoration of the monuments of the Acropolis has been ongoing. The Propylaea was restored between 1909 and 1917, the Erechtheum between 1903 and 1909, the Parthenon from 1897 to 1900 and from 1922 to 1933. The Nike temple was restored a second time shortly before World War II, together with its tower, due to the precarious condition of the latter, thus furnishing an opportunity of confirming the existence of earlier phases of worship on that site.

In the years after World War II, minor restoration and conservation works were carried out. In 1975 a special committee was appointed to study the problems of the Acropolis monuments, largely due to rusting of the iron clamps, ancient and new, corrosion of the surface of the stones by sulphur dioxide and rain, the displacement of architectural members caused by explosions, earthquakes etc. It was clear that drastic measures were called for. The Committee for the Restoration of the Acropolis Monuments, set up in 1977, recommended the immediate commencement of restoration works on the Erechtheum, which was cured of most of its ills and restored between 1979 and 1984.

Panoramic view of the Acropolis
and Lycabettus from
Philopappus hill.

The Propylaea.

MONUMENTS

APPROACH. Several paved paths wend their way to the smooth ascent to the entrance. These were laid a few decades ago for the benefit of visitors, but more or less follow the tracks of the ancient approaches to the Acropolis. In Classical times, when the Propylaea was built (see below), a rather grand roadway was constructed, leading directly up to it from the west, as is evident from the presence of a lateral retaining wall of large, rectangular poros blocks. This is visible just behind the Beulé gate (see below), between it and the pedestal of Agrippa. It appears that the entire slope, to well below the Beulé gate, comprised a ramp, primarily to facilitate the ascent of the considerable crowds of men and beasts participating in the procession of the Panathenaea. About half way along this incline, actually within the Beulé gate, a much earlier retaining wall of polygonal masonry is preserved, attesting the existence of a ramp here, for the convenience of pilgrims, long before Classical times. It is clear from the masonry that it was built in the 6th century BC, most probably in connection with the reorganization of the Great Panathenaea in 566 BC.

BEULÉ GATE. The Beulé gate, thus named after the French archaeologist who excavated it around the middle of the last century, is one of the two entrances to the Acropolis still in use today (the other, modern one, is located just below the Nike tower). This fortress-like structure, built to ensure the safety of the sacred rock after Athens had been laid waste by the Herulae in AD 267, comprises the gateway proper, flanked by two towers. Even from casual inspection, it is obvious that the Beulé gate is constructed of architectural members deriving from other buildings; those destroyed by the Herulae. Of particular interest are the members from the late 5th-century BC choregic monument of Nicias, which stood on the south slope of the Acropolis, near the Theatre of Dionysos.

PEDESTAL OF AGRIPPA. The tall pedestal (almost 10 m.) of grey-blue Hymettan marble, standing near the northwest wing of the Propylaea, is known as the pedestal of Agrippa because at one time a bronze quadriga, driven by Agrippa, son-in-law of the Roman Emperor Augustus, had been set upon it. It has now been confirmed that the charioteer of the original quadriga atop the pedestal was the King of Pergamon, Eumenes II (2nd century BC) and that his figure was later replaced by that of Agrippa.

PROPYLAEA. The Propylaea is a truly magnificent and fitting entrance to the Acropolis. As its name indicates, this is a monumental gateway to the sanctuary. Designed by the architect Mnesicles (who lived in the 5th century BC and was a contemporary of Pericles), building began immediately after the completion of the Parthenon in 438 BC. Work continued until 432 BC but was stopped as the outbreak of the Peloponnesian War seemed imminent. There are grounds for believing that most of the construction had in fact been completed by then and that certain details remained to be finished. Thus, on some of the external walls, particularly on the east face of the so-called Pinakotheke (see below), the lifting bosses, the projections left on the ashlar blocks to facilitate their transportation and positioning have never been removed. Similarly, the finishing process has not been applied on several walls, e.g. the niches formed at the junction of the antae and the side wings of the building's interior, as well as on its exterior (see below).

The floors have not been given their final treatment in many places, e.g. around the column bases.

The building of the Propylaea is a larger and more elaborate version of the old type of Greek propylon, intended to create an impression of grandeur on those approaching the Sanctuary of the Acropolis. It comprises a main building and two wings, projecting to the west, ready to receive the visitor. On the façade of the left wing, the northwest, which faces south, is a small stoa of three Doric columns, behind which is the entrance with two windows on both sides. It was in this chamber, known as the Pinakotheke, that the traveller Pausanias (2nd century AD) reports seeing paintings, including works by the famous 5th-century BC artist, Polygnotos from Thasos.

The right, southwest wing, though symmetrically placed in relation to the northwest, is much smaller. Here too there is a stoa of three Doric columns on the northward-facing façade, but there is no room behind, and the end west wall of the wing has been reduced to a single anta, the sole purpose of which is aesthetic, since it corresponds with the anta of the northwest wing opposite. The obvious reason for the curtailment of the southwest wing is the difficulty of intruding into the area devoted to the Sanctuary of Athena Nike, though perhaps reaction of a political nature from the conservative faction which supported the old cults such as that of Athena Nike, was a contributory factor.

Two sections of the central building of the Propylaea can be distinguished: a west and an east one, which are at different levels; the east is five steps higher, though the internal space is basically uniform. The east section - depth 24 m. - is deeper than the west. Its façade is embellished with a stoa of six Doric columns, taller and stouter than those of the wings. There is an architectural innovation in the interior of the west section of the main building: the roof is supported by two rows of three tall Ionic columns instead of Doric ones, which is the norm in the interior of Doric edifices. Five openings lead into the east section of the main building: a large central portal and two smaller doorways on either side. All the openings narrow towards the top and were closed by heavy wooden leaves. The marble investment of the jambs, seen today, dates from Roman imperial times. The steps are of dark grey Eleusinian marble. The coffers of the marble ceiling used to be painted in vivid col-

The southeast corner of
the temple of
Athena Nike.

ours, with a deep blue and gold star at the centre.

Above the columns on the outer faces of the main building, both the east and the west, was the typical arrangement of triglyphs and plain metopes and there were two pediments, also undecorated. The split-level placement of the main building necessitated the addition of a west pediment on the eastern section, though this was actually half hidden behind the mass of the west section.

It is known from Pausanias and other sources that there were *ex votos* and statues both inside and around the Propylaea. The most renowned of these was the famous Hermes Propylaeos by the sculptor Alcamenes, pupil of Phidias. This had the schema of a Hermaic stele and its type is known from numerous copies. There was also a marble statue of a triple Hecate, also a work of Alcamenes, and a relief of the Graces, by a certain Socrates evidently a namesake of the famous philosopher, who lived somewhat earlier.

TEMPLE OF ATHENA NIKE. The small Ionic temple on top of the tower located to the southwest of the Propylaea was dedicated to Athena Nike. From an inscription of 448 BC it is known that its architect was Callicrates - one of the architects of the Parthenon. There is reason to believe, however, that work did not progress at that time, and that the little temple was actually built much later, between 425 and 421 BC, that is towards the end of the first phase of the Peloponnesian War, shortly before the negotiation of the Peace of Nicias (421 BC).

Between 1935 and 1940 it was decided to pull down the Nike temple and tower, due to the precarious state of the latter, with the intention of consolidating and rebuilding them. It was then ascertained that the temple was in fact the final phase in a very long story. In Mycenaean times the spur of the Acropolis on which the Nike temple was subsequently erected was very heavily fortified, as part of the Cyclopean wall which surrounded the rock. Its purpose was to reinforce the defence of the Acropolis from attack by enemies intent on breaching the main gateway, which was located in the same general area as the Propylaea now stands. The tower has an especial advantage in that it allowed the defenders of the rock to attack the foe's exposed right flank. A small, two-apse shrine, discovered on the west face of the tower in the course of its dismantling, (nowadays behind the similar con-

struction at the west edge of the reconstructed Classical tower), also dates from the Mycenaean period. Pilgrims to the Acropolis evidently deposited their humble offerings here.

The main focus of worship in Archaic times was 1.20 m. below the level of the present temple where an *eschar* (altar for chthonic cult) with a central concavity full of stylized clay figurines has been found. The *eschar* was later enclosed within a small stone temple in the form of a simple *oikos,* two courses of which are preserved. Associated with this *naiskos* is the poros altar discovered to the east of it, bearing a dedicatory inscription of one Patrocles and dated, on the basis of the lettering, to the mid-6th century BC.

The final phase of worship on this site is represented by Callicrates' temple, built entirely of Pentelic marble in the Ionic order. The temple is amphiprostyle, with four slender, monolithic Ionic columns at the front and back. Above the epistyle runs the frieze of finely-worked reliefs: represented on the east frieze (original) is the assembly of the gods around the enthroned Zeus and Poseidon, and on the other sides, the greater part of which are copies of the originals in the British Museum (just a few sections are original), battles between Greeks and Persians or Greeks and Greeks. The portal to the cella is flanked by two jambs, and the openings between these and the lateral walls of the temple were closed in antiquity by a railed fence, thus admitting as much light as possible to the interior, which was somewhat obscured by the height and volume of the nearby Propylaea.

The cult statue in the temple was of wood *(xoanon).* From a description by the 2nd-century BC traveller Heliodoros, the goddess evidently held a pomegranate in her right hand and a helmet in the left. It seems that initially only Nike was worshipped here (not the deity with the symbolic significance she acquired later), a chthonic deity who, in the course of time came to be identified with the much more powerful Athena, the lady of the Acropolis. Since neither the chthonic Nike nor Athena are portrayed with wings, the absence of this attribute from the statue was evidently remarked upon in later times, giving rise to the legend that the Athenians had purposely depicted the goddess wingless to prevent her from flying away and leaving them. Thus the name Wingless Victory (Apteros Nike) prevailed.

Only a few plaques of the marble altar, on which, ac-

The Parthenon from the
\southwest. In the foreground
the Herodeion and
the Stoa of Eumenes.

cording to a 4th-century BC inscription, "One of the most beautiful" heifer calves was sacrificed during the Panathenaea, have survived, towards the Cyclopean wall.

The edge of the tower was protected by a marble parapet about one and a half metres high, bearing relief representations on its exterior: *Nikai* decorating a trophy, or leading bull calves to sacrifice, or performing the sacrifice, as well as three figures of seated Athenas. Many fragments of the parapet have survived, some of which are exhibited in the Acropolis Museum.

The temple stood virtually intact until 1686. In that fateful year, as the Venetian army under Morosini was preparing to invade Athens, the Turkish defenders of the Acropolis pulled it down in order to use the building material to reinforce a bastion erected in the strategically vital position extending from the Nike tower to the pedestal of Agrippa and the Pinakotheke of the Propylaea. After the liberation of the Acropolis from the Turks, Bavarian architects and archaeologists supervising the demolition of the bastion recovered the ancient material and reconstructed the temple. A century later the Greek Archaeological Service, realizing, as we have said, that the tower was in an unstable state, decided to dismantle the temple yet again and rebuild it and the tower in order to consolidate their statics. Thus the tower and temple were taken apart and then restored just before the outbreak of World War II.

East of the Nike temple, at a distance of some 15 m. is an impressive section of the Mycenaean ("Cyclopean") defensive wall, orientated NE-SW. This rampart, which is almost 6 m. thick, is constructed of huge, irregular boulders with smaller stones in the interstices.

On the south wall of the southwest wing of the Propylaea, touching the Cyclopean wall, and in the angle formed by this wing and the main building, remnants of an antecedent Propylon are preserved. After the battle of Marathon the very ancient Mycenaean entrance to the Acropolis was pulled down and a monumental marble Propylon began to be erected in its stead. This was destroyed even before it was completed, by the Persians in 480 BC. Repair works commenced under Cimon, but in 437 BC most of the structure was demolished to make room for Mnesicles' monumental Propylaea.

BRAURONEION AND CHALKOTHEKE.

On passing through the east stoa of the Propylaea the massive Parthenon looms before one, in three-quarter view. In ancient times, however, its lower part was hidden behind other buildings which stood towards the south wall of the Acropolis. The first of these, virtually contiguous with the south-east corner of the Propylaea, was the Sanctuary of Brauronian Artemis, the so-called Brauroneion. Peisistratos had introduced the cult of Artemis to Athens, from the goddess' homeland, the village of Brauron on the east coast of Attica, in the 6th century BC. According to extant inscriptions, expectant mothers dedicated garments and ornaments in the Acropolis sanctuary, in supplication for a safe confinement. The sanctuary was Π-shaped, arranged around an outdoor area, its back set against the south rampart of the Acropolis. The west stoa of the Brauroneion reached as far as the Cyclopean wall. The cuts in the rock for the foundations and some of the blocks of the foundation course of the east stoa are still *in situ.* There were two statues of Artemis in the sanctuary in the 4th century BC: an old *xoanon,* to which the women made their offerings, which depicted the goddess seated, and a marble statue, sculpted by Praxiteles. The *xoanon* was a copy of that in Brauron which, tradition related, had been dedicated by Iphigenia during her journey to the Taurus peninsula. Archaeologists believe that the second statue was of the Artemis Gavion type, known from a later copy in the Louvre, which portrays the goddess walking and adjusting her garment on the shoulder.

East of the Brauroneion are the ruins of a long, narrow rectangular building, the back face of which, like the Brauroneion, abutted onto the south wall of the Acropolis, and which had a porticoed façade. This is generally believed to have been the "Chalkotheke", in which bronze *(chalkos) ex votos* and vessels were stored.

PARTHENON. The largest and most impressive of all the edifices on the Acropolis is the Parthenon. From whatever direction one approaches Athens it is visible from afar, and long before one passes through the eastern colonnade of the Propylaea its imposing presence fills one with awe and wonder. An enormous project by the standards of Greek antiquity, the building of the Parthenon is due to a happy coincidence of several favourable factors:

The Parthenon from the west.

The northeast corner of the
entablature of the Parthenon.

1) The personality of the man who proposed it, Pericles. Pericles was not merely an adroit politician who, through his outstanding abilities managed, within a complex democratic body politic zealously guarded by a difficult people, to direct the fortunes of Athens for two decades, he was also a visionary and an intellectual figure of rare stature. Pericles wished to erect in place of the half-finished Parthenon destroyed by the Persians, a new temple which, not only by virtue of its larger dimensions but also its inspiration, would be the incarnation of Athens' glorious past, its power, its cultural pre-eminence. A monument to the glorification of the patron goddess and the aggrandizement of past achievements, as well as to the splendour of life in the Athens of the day.

2) Pericles' select and stimulating circle of friends, with whom he was in close and continual contact, included the philosopher Anaxagoras, the poet Sophocles, the musician Damon, his mistress, the lovely Aspasia, and, above all, the sculptor and painter Phidias. It is perhaps to Phidias that the Parthenon owes the magnificence of its conception, since it is known from the literary sources that his artistic character was admired for its "grandeur" and "divinity". Certainly the completion of the Parthenon is due to Phidias' exceptional organization of the construction team, the perfect division of labour of a veritable army of artists, artisans, builders and ordinary manual workers, extolled centuries later by Plutarch in his *Life of Pericles,* for according to him, Phidias was the one "who arranged everything and supervised everything".

3) The third, but equally important factor is economic. Athens' hegemony of the anti-Persian league, achieved just a few years after its formation in 477 BC, secured unparalleled affluence for the city, facilitating the execution of public works. Its resources for such projects were considerably increased when, after 454 BC, the treasury of the League was transferred, on the pretext of greater security, from Delos to Athens. By a decree of the *demos* it was decided that the 1/60th of the allies' contributions which had hitherto been given to Delian Apollo be paid into the treasury of Athens, that is the public purse. Thus large sums of money from the League fund were disbursed for the beautification of the Acropolis and Athens, despite the objections of conservative politicians, whom Pericles managed to remove entirely from the political arena.

From 447 BC hundreds of men worked non-stop on a gigantic, well-planned and highly organized project; the building and decoration of the Parthenon and the construction of the precious chryselephantine cult statue. Plutarch mentions masons, sculptors, bronze-smiths, stone-carvers, gilders, modellers in ivory, painters of all kinds and many others. The temple was inaugurated in 438 BC, on the goddess' birthday, although work on the pediments was not completed until six years later, on the very eve of the Peloponnesian War.

The Parthenon (length 69.50 m. x width 30.86 m.), though the most perfect architectural creation in the Doric order, is not the most representative, since its proportions are somewhat different and certain of its elements derive from the Ionic order. For example, its expansive aspect is unusual for Doric temples and the addition of the frieze, albeit inside the outer colonnade around the main building, is an Ionic influence, as are the four Ionic columns supporting the roof in the chamber at the rear of the temple, that known as the "Parthenon".

All the dimensions of the building are based on a precisely calculated system of rations and proportions which, thanks to the equally well-calculated deviations and refinements avoid creating a cold and lifeless impression, but on the contrary imbue it with an aura of vitality. Mathematical calculations had been widely applied in Greek architecture in earlier times, though nowhere on such a scale and nowhere with such refined relationships as on the Parthenon. For instance, the diminution and entasis of the columns and vertical planes, which had also been applied earlier, achieve their culmination in this edifice where they are more discreet than ever before yet more apparent than in subsequent Doric edifices. The famous curvature of the horizontal planes of the building, the crepidoma and even the entablature, in conjunction with its sense of breadth, give the impression that the temple is breathing deeply within the site.

It is impossible, and in any case beyond the scope of this short account, not only to analyse, but even to describe the architectural refinements of the Parthenon, thanks to which this building ranks as one of man's greatest achievements. Here we confine ourselves to pointing out the role once played by sculpture in the building's decoration.

Originally - and even today - all those surfaces of the

The southwest corner of the
entablature with part of the
columns.

Parthenon susceptible to embellishment, that is the metopes, frieze and pediments, bore sculpted decoration.

There were 92 metopes all around the outside of the building. Depicted on those of the east side - most of which have nowadays been removed in order to prevent further erosion - was the Gigantomachy. On the metopes of the west side - all still *in situ* but badly damaged - was the Amazonomachy. Those of the north side showed the fall of Troy. Here too the plaques are *in situ,* excepting those destroyed when the building was blown up by a shell fired by Morosini. Most of these metopes are badly effaced, though the last one towards the west, the northwest, is reasonably well-preserved and portrays a seated female figure, before whom stands another female. This was dubbed the "Annunciation" in Christian times, which may explain why it has survived in a better state than the rest. The metopes of the south side are in quite good condition, except the middle ones which were lost in the Morosini explosion. Represented on the end ones is the Centauromachy, that is the struggle between the Lapiths and equine Centaurs who tried to ravish their womenfolk and children at the nuptial feast of the Lapith King, Peirithoos. Most of these metopes are in the British Museum, one, the southwest, is still *in situ,* one is displayed in the Acropolis Museum, while two others and a great number of fragments are in its storeroom.

The narrow sides of the building were surmounted by pediments with splendid compositions of sculptures in the round. Pausanias says a few words on the subjects of these, though a great deal more is known from sketches made by Carrey, a short while before the destruction of the Parthenon by Morosini. Depicted on the east pediment was the birth of Athena from the head of Zeus, in the presence of the assembled gods, while in the angles were the chariot of Helios emerging from the waters of the Ocean, left, and the chariot of Selene plunging into the waters, right. Phidias endowed this old myth with a new universal yet symbolic meaning. It encapsulated the birth of a new era, the age of Athenian wisdom and might.

Represented on the west pediment was the quarrel between Poseidon and Athena over their claim to dominance over Attica. All the gods and heroes of the region were present.

Of the 50 or so enormous statues comprising the two compositions, only 11 have survived. Most of them are in the British Museum and a few are in the Acropolis Museum. They are the loveliest works ever to have been fashioned by ancient Greek sculptors. As has been said before, the temple was surrounded by a Doric colonnade, while the ceiling of this stoa was adorned with painted stone coffers. The ceilings in the other parts of the temple were of wood and thus all traces have been lost. The roof consisted of marble tiles, many of which have survived.

Around the top of the external wall of the temple proper was a relief frieze. Its subject did not derive from the world of myth, as is the case for the other sculpted parts of the temple (the metopes and pediments), but from an actual event in the life of Athens at the time. It illustrated the procession of the Panathenaea, the festival held to mark the goddess' birthday on the 28th day of the month Hecatombai on (July - August). The purpose of the procession was to carry the peplos, woven during the past year by the so-called Arrephoroi (young girls from aristocratic families of Athens), from the lower city to the Acropolis, where it was handed over to the priests, which act was followed by the sacrifice of one hundred oxen on the altar of Athena. On the frieze the subject has been realistically rendered with regard to details of the participants, but there is no reference to landscape, as if the procession was taking place in an idealized setting. Moreover, the procession, which commences on the west face and then divides into two sections, one on the north and one on the south side, meets on the east face, where the gods await its arrival, unseen guests sitting comfortably and conversing among themselves. Apart from the west frieze, which is *in situ* on the building, a few plaques are housed in the Acropolis Museum, the greater part is in the British Museum, one plaque from the east side is in the Louvre and one in the Vienna Museum.

The interior of the temple was divided into a prodomos, the temple proper, called the "hekatompedon naos", the Parthenon proper and the opisthodomos. In front of the prodomos and the opisthodomos, but behind the external colonnade, was a second row of six Doric columns, between which there were railings in antiquity, to protect the precious *ex votos* kept within.

The prodomos led into the temple proper, which was arranged as an elongated Π by a twin colonnade of

Doric columns. On a magnificent pedestal at the far end of the chamber stood the enormous chryselephantine cult statue of Athena, a creation of Phidias. Nothing has remained of this work, since it was removed from here by the Christians, perhaps to be taken to Constantinople. There, tradition (somewhat confused) relates that it was consumed by fire shortly afterwards. Its type is known from a small marble statue in the National Archaeological Museum, Athens, found on the site now occupied by the Varvakeion, which replicates it: the standing goddess has an air of serene sanctity. She is clad in a Doric peplos, girdled at the waist, and a wide *aegis* covers her chest. On her head is an elaborately embellished Attic helmet with a sphinx in the middle and a pegasus to left and right (Pausanias describes these as griffins). Her left arm rests on the angle of her shield, which touches the ground, and in her extended right hand she proffers a Nike. The outer face of the shield was decorated with a relief representation of the Amazonomachy, the inner face with the Gigantomachy. Depicted in relief on the high soles of her sandals was the Centauromachy and illustrated on the statue's base was the myth of Pandora in gilded relief.

There was no direct access from the main temple to the so-called "Parthenon", which was entered via the opisthodomos. Its roof was upheld by four Ionic columns, of which only traces have remained on the floor. Numerous *ex votos* were kept in this chamber. When the temple was converted into a church several centuries later, the "Parthenon" served as the narthex and its walls were covered with wall-paintings, some remnants of which were still visible until a few years ago.

It was in the opisthodomos which, like the prodomos, was closed by railings, that the city treasury (monies of Athena and of other gods) was kept, in accordance with Callias' decree of 435/34 BC.

With the domination of Christianity, the Parthenon, like many other ancient temples, was transformed into a church. When exactly it was put to this new usage is not known, though it was probably quite late, since Athens persisted in its faith in the ancient gods for many years. The entrance to the church was from the west, since the sanctuary was in its east part. The "Parthenon" became the narthex, the partition between it and the temple proper was dispensed with and the east side arranged as the sanctuary apse. It

seems that it was in the process of this alteration that the central part of the scene on the east pediment was destroyed. Much changed, the Parthenon was dedicated to Aghia Sophia (Holy Wisdom) and at some time its walls were decorated with wall-paintings.

When the Franks entered Athens in 1204 the "Great Church of Athens", as the Parthenon was then known, was consecrated to the Latin dogma and renamed Notre Dame. It was perhaps then (or possibly earlier) that windows were opened in the walls, in order to better illuminate the interior, thus destroying sections of the frieze.

After Athens' capture by the Turks in 1456, the Parthenon, was transformed into a mosque, and a minaret, the lower part of which still survives, was built on the southwest side of the opisthodomos.

Up until the 17th century the greater part of the Classical decoration was preserved *in situ.* Mention has already been made in the historical outline of the sketches made shortly after 1674 by Jacques Carrey, and of the damage the building suffered in 1687 due to the explosion of the powder-store housed therein, when it was struck by a shell from Morosini's artillery. Not long afterwards the Turks built a small mosque on top of the ruins of the Parthenon.

In the many drawings and descriptions of travellers who visited Athens and the Acropolis in the 18th century, the Parthenon is shown as it was before being denuded of its sculpted decoration.

As has been said earlier, the great looting of its decoration was carried out in the early years of the 19th century, by the British ambassador to Constantinople, Lord Elgin. Having secured a sultan's firman, he removed and transported to England the greater part of the Parthenon sculptures, one of the Caryatids and other antiquities.

After the creation of the independent state of Modern Greece, the monument was freed of all later additions (though the lower part of the minaret is, as mentioned above, still there), and the little mosque collapsed of its own accord in 1842.

The first restoration works were executed as early as 1841. Interventions on a larger scale were made between 1896 and 1900 and between 1922 and 1933. Restoration works were resumed in 1987 (see historical outline).

EARLIER PARTHENONS. The Periclean Parthenon was not the first temple built on this site. From

close scrutiny of its foundations and of traces on the rock, as well as the study of architectural members and decorative sculptures found in the fill of the Acropolis, archaeological scholarship arrived at the conclusion that a succession of temples had stood on this spot.

1) A first large poros stone temple, possibly built under Peisistratos. German archaeologists named this the Ur-Parthenon, that is the primal Parthenon. It may in fact be the "Hekatompedos Naos" mentioned in inscriptions (and not the "Archaios Naos" which stood a little further northwards).

2) After the battle of Marathon that temple was pulled down and building of a new one, of Pentelic marble, commenced. This had progressed up to the level of the first drums of the colonnade when it was destroyed by the Persian invaders in 480 BC. It is to this temple that the many unworked column drums, some dispersed over the rock and others incorporated in the north defensive wall of the Acropolis, in front of the Erechtheum, belong, as well as other broken and burnt architectural members.

TEMPLE OF ROMA AND AUGUSTUS. In Roman times a small, circular monopteral temple (i.e. without cella) stood to the east of the Parthenon. Many of its members are preserved *in situ* and its dedicatory inscription, carved in large majuscules on the epistyle, informs us that it was dedicated to the goddess Roma and Caesar Augustus. Thus the building is dated after AD 27, the year Octavian assumed the title of Augustus. Its architectural members bear a strong resemblance to those of the Erechtheum and were evidently directly influenced by them.

ERECHTHEUM. The Erechtheum is one of the most peculiar and complex temples of antiquity. Its deviations from the canonical schema were dictated by several reasons: the need to unite the most ancient and revered "signs" with the other sacred places which abound in this part of the rock; the chthonic cult practised in at least one part of the building; as well as the considerable difference in the height of the rock, which is 3.50 m. higher in the east than in the west part.

The temple's basic plan is, of course, a long narrow rectangle, the norm for all temples. However, two porches project from this module, asymmetrically positioned on the north and south side and, moreover, different from one another. Furthermore, the east part of the edifice is a regular prostyle temple, while the west part is a two-storeyed building with a stoa on the upper section of the west face.

The name Erechtheum is a later one. It is encountered only twice, once in the account of the traveller Pausanias and once in Pseudo-Plutarch, while in official inscriptions of 409/8 BC a periphrastic description is given: "the temple in the city in which is the ancient statue", and in the inscriptions of the treasuries of Athens and in Strabo it is called either the "temple of Polias" or the "archaios naos".

When viewed from its east face the Erechtheum looks like a regular Ionic prostyle temple with six beautiful columns. Today its interior is a single space and presents a most confusing picture, for in the 7th century AD the building was converted into a church and the inside was excavated down to the foundations. However, in ancient times this was divided into two sections, one to the fore, the east, and one at the rear, the west, between which, as in the Parthenon, there was no communication. The east section was dedicated to the cult of Athena Polias. Here was housed the old "heaven-sent" xoanon, which was of olive wood. It also contained a gold lamp, work of the famous sculptor Callimachos, which was filled with oil only once a year, and a host of votive offerings.

The west section was the "Erechtheum" proper, that is the chamber dedicated to the cult of Erechtheus, a prehistoric deity whom, according to one tradition, Zeus had slain with a thunderbolt, and who gradually came to be identified with the more powerful god, Poseidon. This was entered through the northwest porch, the roof of which is supported by a Π- shaped arrangement of six Ionic columns with richly decorated capitals and bases. The marble coffers of the ceiling are painted and adorned with appliqué metal ornaments. Set in the floor was an altar, onto which tiny loaves of sweet bread were cast. These fell through an internal opening (nowadays there is a gap in the floor) onto the rock, where there were the marks left by Poseidon's trident (or according to another version Zeus's thunderbolt with which he had killed Erechtheus). The corresponding coffer on the ceiling was left open, to indicate the direction of its trajectory. The doorway leading to the vestibule was also elaborately decorated, though part of the ornament-

ation seen today is from repairs made in Roman times. Under the floor of the vestibule was the famous "Erechthean Sea" (or "well"), that is the salt water which had gushed forth when Poseidon struck the rock with his trident.

Also in the west section were altars to Poseidon and Erechtheus, to Hephaestus and to the hero Boutos.

At the west corner of the south wall stands the charming porch of the Korai (the Caryatids as they are more commonly known), which is in effect a small balcony onto the processional way followed by the Panathenaea. The Caryatids are six statues of maidens placed in Π-shaped formation (those on the building today are copies of the originals, four of which are exhibited in the Acropolis Museum). Beneath the floor of the porch was the tomb of the mythical king of Athens, Cecrops.

The west wall of the Erechtheum is two-storeyed. The upper storey, which corresponds with the level of the north porch, was originally arranged as an open stoa with four columns joined at the bottom by a parapet. When the building was repaired in the 1st century BC these columns were incorporated in the wall and the openings converted into windows, which can be seen today.

Building of the Erechteum evidently began during the interval of the Peace of Nicias (421 BC). It is apparent from a valuable inscription of 409/8 BC that works had been interrupted for quite some time and were resumed in that year. The most likely reason for this interruption is the Sicilian Campaign (415 BC), and for their resumption the ephemeral Athenian victories after 410 BC. The architect of the second phase of construction was one Philocles, cited in the inscription but unknown from other sources. The project was completed in 406 BC. It is known from Xenophon that in that same year the nearby old temple of Athena (see below) was badly damaged by fire, and it would seem that it was then that the old *xoanon* of the goddess was transferred to the newly-built temple.

At some time in the Early Christian period the building was transformed into a church and radical alterations were made to its interior to serve the needs of the new religion. Under the Turks the garrison commander installed his family here; his own residence was in the Propylaea. At the begining of the 19th century Lord Elgin removed one of the caryatids and some architectural members, which he took to England, along with the Parthenon sculptures. During the Greek War of Independence, when Kiutahi besieged the Greek defenders of the Acropolis in 1827, part of the south wall fell down, together with the Caryatids.

In the 19th century, restoration work was undertaken on several parts of the building. The porch of the caryatids was reconstructed and the figure removed by Lord Elgin replaced by a copy sent by the British Museum. Systematic restoration was carried out between 1902 and 1909 by N. Balanos. A monumental publication of the temple was published in 1927 by the American School of Classical Studies. Between 1979 and 1984 the temple was restored once again, and the caryatids were removed from the porch to salvage them from further corrosion.These are now on display in the Acropolis Museum and have been replaced by copies on the building.

In front of the west side of the Erechtheum was the Sanctuary of Pandrosos, within which was the sacred olive tree of Athena. At the beginning of the century Queen Sophia planted an olive tree on this very spot

"ARCHAIOS NAOS" OR "DÖRPFELD'S TEMPLE". Visible to the south of the Erechtheum are the foundations of a temple (part of these are actually under the south wall of the Erechtheum). This was the "Archaios Naos" of Athena in which her "heaven-sent" *xoanon* was housed until 406 BC. It was a rectangular building comprising two sections: an eastern, one dedicated to the worship of Athena, which, as was usual for the cellas of ancient temples, was divided into three parts by two rows of columns, and a western one, dedicated to the worship of Poseidon, absolutely separate from the other, entered from the west side and consisting of three chambers. This lay-out is exactly the same as that of the Erechtheum, the schema of which was greatly influenced by it. Perhaps no other temple on the Acropolis has preoccupied archaeologists as much as this one. Certainly no other has had such a divisive effect. The period in which it was built, its phases, the duration of its use and its decoration, are all issues on which there is anything but a consensus of views. Though the dating of its foundations to the 6th century BC is not doubt-

ed, because those of the temple proper are of different material from those of the external colonnade, the first scholar to study the building systematically, Dörpfeld (by whose name it is conventionally known today), thought, like other colleagues, that it had been built in two phases: in the first the main temple and in the second the external colonnade. Schuchhardt, on the other hand, maintained that despite the difference in the material of the foundations, the temple had had its "ample" dimensions from the outset. This is the view which has tended to prevail.

Nevertheless there are considerable differences of opinion among archaeologists as to the temple's sculpted decoration, which was certainly initially of poros (apart from the central *acroterion*, the Gorgoneion, and the sima which were of marble. See below in the chapter on the Museum).

In the time of the Peisistratids, however, *circa* 520 BC, the decoration was renewed and executed entirely of marble (see chapter on the Museum, gallery V). Like the other buildings on the Acropolis, the temple was destroyed by the Persians in 480 BC. After the Persian Wars it was repaired (probably without the external colonnade) to house the statue of the goddess (which the Athenians had evidently taken with them when the city was vacated in 480 BC) and to be used once more as the treasury of the city, until the Parthenon was built and it was transferred there. As has been said above, the temple was destroyed by fire in 406 BC. Little is known of its subsequent fate. Some scholars think that it was repaired and maintained, since there is - unclear - information in Demosthenes (mid-4th century BC) of a fire in the opisthodomos. We are, however, completely in the dark as to whether it was in fact repaired again or not. Nevertheless, it should be pointed out that its presence would have completely obscured the south face of the Erechtheum.

ARREPHORION. A few metres northwest of the Erechtheum are the foundations of a small, temple-shaped building of poros, thought to have been the residence of the Arrephoroi. These maidens were entrusted with the task of weaving the peplos for Athena and performing certain mystical rites during the summer to ensure a good harvest.

EX VOTOS. The *ex votos* set up on the Acropolis after the Persian destruction have been lost *in toto*, but

The Erechtheum. View
from the southeast.

The Erechtheum. The porch
with the *korai*
from the southeast.

Cooper-plate engraving.
The Erechtheum from the southwest.

the many cuttings preserved in the rock, and occasional remnants of their bases, are tangible evidence of their presence. Pausanias mentions them, and the combination of his testimony with the actual traces enables us to recognize where they were placed.

Approximately 40 m. east of the Propylaea, fragments of the base of a colossal bronze statue of Athena Promachos are preserved. The statue, which was a work of Phidias, has not survived. It was evidently taken to Constantinople, where it was destroyed by the mob in the turmoil before the city's capture by the Franks in 1204. A general idea of its appearance may be gained from Athenian coins of the Roman period and small bronze statuettes which imitate its type. The goddess was standing, her spear resting on the ground but its tip so positioned that it glinted in the sun and was thus espied by all those approaching Piraeus from Sounion, since the statue was extremely tall. In her right hand she held an owl.

Set up in the vicinity of the pedestal of the Promachos was a bronze quadriga and the chains with which the Athenians had shackled the Boeotians and Chalcideans when they defeated them in 506 BC. This *ex voto* escaped the Persian destruction and two dedicatory inscriptions have survived, one early and one later, of 457 BC, perhaps due to a repair. Proceeding from the Propylaea and skirting the north side of the Parthenon, there is an area of the rock cordoned off by railings. This encloses an inscription of *circa* AD 100 which reads: "Fructiferous Earth according to the prophecy". Adjacent to it is a small levelled surface on which the figure of Gaia (Earth) was represented from the waist upwards, as if emerging from the rock, placed there by the Athenians after a period of drought in fulfilment of a vow.

East of the inscription to Gaia is a small semicircular base, still *in situ,* which bore the portrait statues of two eminent Athenian generals, Conon, victor in the naval battle at Cnidus (394 BC), and his son Timotheos, as cited in the inscription.

Preserved on the rock even further to the east, near the northeast corner of the Parthenon, are the cuttings for the base of the statue of Procne and Itys, which is displayed in the vestibule of the Acropolis Museum (see below).

On the south wall of the Acropolis, near the Muse-

um, stood a large martial *ex voto,* the many-figured sculpted group dedicated by the pro-Athenian king of Pergamon, Attalos II. It depicted mythical battles, the Gigantomachy and the Amazonomachy, and historical battles, those against the Persians and against the Gauls, alluding to the victories of his father, Attalos I. Nowadays only copies of some of the figures have survived, dispersed in museums abroad.

The statue of Athena by the Archaic sculptor Endoios, described and seen by Pausanias, has been identified in a seated sculpture exhibited in the Acropolis Museum (see below).

There was also a statue of a priestess of Athena, Lysimache, on the Acropolis. This was a work of the 5th - 4th century BC sculptor Demetrios, famous for his realism, who portrayed her as an old woman.

The exact position of the portrait statue of Pericles, a work of Phidias's pupil Cresilas and which is described by Pausanias, is not known. A fragment of its base has been found, however, bearing the dedicatory inscription.

Outside the Propylaea and touching the first column from the south, is a circular pedestal, on which a statue of Athena Hygeia once stood, as attested by the inscription which also reveals the name of the sculptor, Pyrrhus. According to tradition the statue was dedicated after an accident which happened during the building of the Propylaea, but, it is more probably connected with the great plague of 429 BC.

In the corresponding position to the left of anyone entering the Acropolis stood the statue of the so-called Athena Lemnia, another of Phidias' creations. This had been dedicated by Athenian lot-holders who left for Lemnos in the middle of the 5th century BC. It is generally believed that the type of the work is rendered in the body of a Roman copy in Dresden and a head in Bologna.

Still standing in the western section of the Brauroneion is an enormous marble base on which stood a gigantic bronze *ex voto,* the Wooden Horse, a work of the sculptor Strongylion. It was set up in the time of the Peloponnesian War.

Section of the north wall of the Acropolis. Modern shelves on which scattered pieces are classified.

From the north frieze of
the Parthenon.

THE MUSEUM

The Acropolis Museum, built in a hollow in the southeast part of the rock, is so unobtrusive that it does not interfere with the ancient monuments and cannot be seen from afar. It was erected in two phases. The front section with porch, designed by the architect Kalkos, was built between 1865 and 1874, and the galleries to the east, planned by the architect S. Karantinos, were added between 1952 and 1955. The exhibits were mainly arranged between 1955 and 1966 by G. Miliadis, who was Director of the Acropolis for many years. In 1979, when the Caryatids were put on display in Gallery IX, Miliadis' lay-out of the exhibits was altered, necessitating minor changes in that of the vestibule also.

Head of a philosopher
of Late Antiquity.
5th century AD.

VESTIBULE

Statue of Procne (no. 1358). The mythical Procne, betrayed wife of the king of Thrace, Tereus, is depicted contemplating the murder of her son Itys in order to avenge her husband. It would appear that this is the statue which Pausanias mentions as standing to the north of the Parthenon. The ancient traveller also adds that it was a votive offering of Alcamenes, a pupil and close colleague of Phidias, and one of the greatest sculptors of the 5th century BC. If the statue of Procne is indeed one of his works, as is believed, then its style is an invaluable guide for the recognition of Alcamenes' hand in other sculpted works. *Circa* 430 BC.

Head of Alexander (no. 1331). An idealized original portait of Alexander as a young man, perhaps sculpted soon after the battle of Chaironeia (338 BC), on the unique occasion Alexander visited Athens. It is usually regarded as a work of Leochares, but stylistically displays closer affinity with the circle of Praxiteles.

Head of a philosopher (no. 1313). A remarkably expressive head from late antiquity (5th century AD), evidently portraying one of the philosophers of the Neo-Platonic School, the dominant intellectual force in Athens at that time.

Head of Alexander.
Circa 338 BC.

Lioness of poros stone.
From the right section of
a large Archaic pediment.

GALLERY I

Architectural sculptures from large and small edifices on the Acropolis in the early 6th century BC.

A lioness rending a calf (no. 4). The right section of the poros pediment of a large temple, in all probability the earliest Parthenon (see chapter on Monuments). An accomplished work of extraordinary impact and excellent technique.

Pediment with Hydra (no.1). This vividly coloured, low relief in poros stone, from a small building on the Acropolis (perhaps a "Treasury"), represents Heracles' extermination of the Lernaean Hydra, in the presence of his friend Iolaos.

Marble head of a Gorgon (no. 701). The head of a running figure of a Gorgon which was the central acroterion of a large, early 6th-century BC temple, possibly the first Parthenon. Clear outlines, marked decorative tendency, sensitive modelling.

GALLERY II

Architectural sculptures and votive statues of the 6th century BC.

Sculpted groups (nos 35 and 36) of *poros* stone from the edges of the pediment of a large Archaic temple: the "archaios naos" according to Schuchhardt, or the second phase of the earliest Parthenon, in Dinsmoor's opinion. In the left section, Heracles in combat with the Triton (no. 36). In the right section (no. 35) a three-bodied winged daemon with lower body of entwined snakes. The objects held in their hands are regarded as symbolic manifestations of the elemental forces of nature (air, water, fire). A work of remarkable plasticity and primordial strength, tempered by an expression of deep humanity on the faces of the trimorph. The colours are plain yet bright and well chosen. The composition was surmounted by the marble raking cornice of the temple, adorned with incised and painted palmettes, floral motifs *et al*.

Poros pediment depicting the Apotheosis of Heracles (no. 9). This piece, from a small building, shows Heracles being received on Mount Olympus and his deification. Its monumentality and vigour are enhanced by the lavish use of colour. *Circa* 580-570 BC.

Moschophoros (Calf-bearer) (no. 624). A Hymettan marble votive statue of an Athenian aristocrat, clad in a close-fitting chiton and holding a calf on his shoulders, an offering to the goddess. The name preserved on the base, read from right to left, is Rombos or Combos. Firmly modelled smooth surfaces, wide-open eyes (originally inlaid), a controlled yet mirthful smile. *Circa* 570 BC.

The so-called Olive or Troilus pediment (no.52), of poros stone. The piece comes from a small edifice erected in *circa* 570 BC. It is unusual that a building is represented with a tree (olive?) incised beside it. The female emerging from the building appears to be carrying a *hydria* of water, other figures stand or move outside. It has been suggested that it depicts the ambush Achilles set for Troilus, son of Priam, when he went to water his horses at the fountain.

Headless kore (no. 593) of white marble. The earliest of the Acropolis korai. Her hieratic motionless stance is emphasized by the soft planes of her garments, devoid of undulation. In her left hand, brought onto her chest, she holds a pomegranate, and in the lowered right one a wreath. *Circa* 580 - 570 BC.

White marble quadriga (no. 577). Only the forequarters of the horses are rendered, *en face*, the heads of the two middle ones turned inwards and of those at either side, outwards. The charioteer, may be imagined in the background, also shown frontally. *Circa* 570 BC.

Two marble horses from a
votive quadriga. Frontal
view. *Circa* 570 BC.

The right edge of the
pediment of the large
Archaic temple. Poros
three- bodied Daemon.
Circa 560 BC.

Votive statue
of a
Moschophoro
(Calf-bearer).
Circa 570 BC.

Kore no. 593.
Circa 570 BC.

Poros head of a bull
from a pedimental
composition representing
two lions attacking a bull.

GALLERY III

Sculptures and architectural reconstitutions of buildings from the Archaic Acropolis.

Two lions lacerating a bull (no.3). This poros stone sculpture belongs to the central section of the pediment of a large temple, possibly the same pediment as that with the compositions of Heracles and the Triton, and the Trimorph (Gallery II). In comparison with the lioness in Gallery I, the realism is more pronounced, especially in the expressive force of the ferocious felines and the suffering of the bull.

Statue of a kore (no. 619). A Naxian work in Naxian marble. First half of the 6th century BC.

Upper body of a similar Naxian kore (no. 677), likewise of Naxian marble. The head is preserved. Slightly later in date than no. 619. *Circa* 560 BC.

Lower part of an enthroned female figure (no. 618). A notable work in white marble, dated to 520 BC.

Reconstitutions of small stone edifices of the 6th century BC are displayed in this gallery.

Votive sphinx, 540 - 530 BC.

Lion-head waterspout
of the later phase of the
"Archaios Naos" of Athena.
Circa 520 BC.

GALLERY IV

Marble sculpture of the Late Archaic period, particularly *ex votos* (korai, equestrian figures etc.).
White marble relief of Athena receiving adorers (no. 581). Athena, a figure of exquisite sensitivity, receives a family bringing her an offering of a pig. The pronounced Archaic traits are characteristic of a
fin de siecle archaicizing tendency.
Lower body of a white marble statue of Athena (no. 136), clad in a close-fitting chiton. The hole beside her foot was obviously to receive her spear. The figure stands on a calyx-shaped column capital,
the ornamentation of which is conspicuously coloured. The delicacy of the modelling and natural
tread of the foot are quite wonderful. *Circa* 500 BC.
The Rampin horseman (no. 590). This sculpture fragment in island marble comes from an imposing
ex voto which initially included two horsemen. Part of one and his steed are preserved, and a few
pieces of the second horse. The head of the surviving horseman is not the original; this is in the
Louvre Museum, and once belonged to the Rampin collection, hence the name. Whereas the rider's
head, bows slightly and turns left, that of the horse is inclined in the opposite direction, right. The
horseman's highly stylized hair is extremely finely executed and his radiant smile replete with humanity. The body is robust and very simple. Interpretation of the piece is difficult. The wreath of oak-
leaves signifies that the horseman was a victor, though it is not known in which contest. Perhaps the
work is, as has been suggested, an *ex voto* representing the sons of the tyrant Peisistratus, who were

victorious in some horse race. It is dated on stylistic grounds to the middle of the 6th century BC and is undoubtedly the work of an artist of the first rank.

Peplophoros (no. 679). This kore owes her name to the unpleated Doric peplos which she wears over an Ionic chiton, visible towards the bottom of the figure. Though the peplos was abandoned in favour of the Ionic chiton as a female garment at about this time (most of the Acropolis korai wear Ionic dress), the peplophoros retains it as a mark of conservatism. There are copious traces of colour on the hair, eyes, clothes and elsewhere. This is a work of a major artist of the day. Despite its simplicity, the modelling of the torso is taut and confident, but above all the adroit rendering of the fresh maid-enly bloom of the face, the firm flesh and compact robustness overall, is quite incredible. *Circa* 530 BC.

Dog (no. 143). This and another dog, of which fragments have been found, stood beside the entrance to the Archaic sanctuary of Brauroneian Artemis. The lean hunting hound seems ready to pounce on its prey. 520 BC.

Lion-head water-spout (no. 69). This architectural member is from the repairs made to the "archaios naos" in 520 BC. The air of vigour and vitality is heightened by the bright colours.

"Persian Horseman" (no. 606). The statue owes its sobriquet to its close-fitting costume embellished with a colourful lozenge pattern, reminiscent of Persian-Scythian dress. Since some consider the garment to be Thracian, the work is alternatively known as Miltiades, after the Athenian general who had lived for several years in Thrace as leader of the Athenian colonists at the end of the 6th century BC. *Circa* 520 BC.

Most of the other *ex votos* in this gallery are korai, attired in the Ionic chiton, over which a small Ionic himation has been diagonally thrown. The garments are now densely pleated and very often there is a hint of movement, as if they were imbued with a life of their own. Quite often the chiton is held in one hand and pulled to the side, raising the hem and thus emphasizing the plasticity of the limbs. This series of later korai dates to 520 - 490 BC. Outstanding among them are:

Kore no. 675. A very small, finely worked statue with a charming smile. The colours are vivid and well-preserved. Some scholars are of the opinion that it is the work of a Chian artist. *Circa* 510 BC.

Kore no. 594, headless. Particularly impressive is the multi-pleated and very delicate raiment with its well-preserved colourful decoration. *Circa* 520 BC.

Heads of korai nos 643, 696. The bodies of these korai have been lost. No. 643 dates to *circa* 510 BC, as apparent from the half-open, blissful eyes and the exceptionally tender modelling, almost alive to the touch.

The second, no. 696, dated ten years later, wears a *polos* on her head. The flesh is firmer and sparse and her expression somewhat contemplative, presaging the Classical spirit.

Kore no. 674 is of approximately the same period. A slim maiden of noble birth, her expression is on the threshold of the artistic inquiries of the Classical age. The work of a pioneering artist.

Kore no. 684. Festive and full of confidence, this kore with her rectangular body and vertical pleats anticipates the structure of the "Severe" style, yet in all other respects retains the traits of Archaic art. *Circa* 490 BC.

In addition to the korai, the following works are worthy of attention.

"Endoios' Athena" (no. 625). This headless statue with its badly eroded surface was found on the north slope of the Acropolis. In all probability this is the statue of Athena by the famous 6th-century BC sculptor Endoios, which Pausanias reports seeing on the Acropolis in the 2nd century AD. Thus this lively inspired work is one of the few which survived the Persian destruction.

The so-called
Lampin Horseman.
An ex voto of the
d- 6th century BC.
e head is a plaster
py of the original,
h is in the Louvre.

The "Peplophoros"
kore, no. 679.
Circa 530 BC.

Head of a sphinx (?),
no. 654. *Circa* 560 BC.

Ex voto of a dog.
Circa 520 BC.

The "Lyons kore",
no.269.
Circa
550 - 540 BC.

Votive relief of Hermes and
the Graces, no. 702.
Late 6th century BC.

Relief plaque with
representation of a charioteer.
Late 6th century BC.

Kore no. 670.
Circa 510 BC.

Kore no. 6
A Chian w
Circa 510 F

ore no. 673.
Circa
20 - 510 BC.

Head no. 696.
Circa 500 BC.

Head no. 643.
Circa 510 BC.

Athena and a Giant from the pediment showing the battle of Gods and Giants, dating from the later phase of the "Archaios Naos" (circa 520 BC).

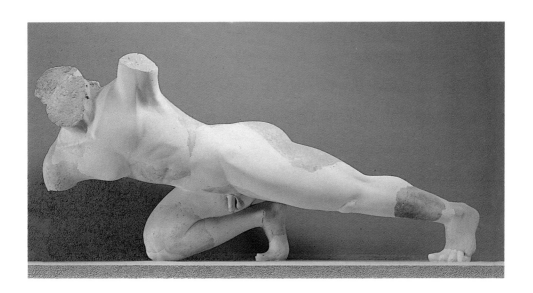

GALLERY V

This gallery is dominated by the pediment of the "Archaios Naos" of Athena, recently dated to *circa* 505 BC (it had been previously dated to 520 BC), though other works representative of the main artistic trends in Archaic sculpture during the final quarter of the 6th century BC are also displayed.

Pediment with the Gigantomachy, from the "Archaios Naos" of Athena (no. 631). At the centre Athena, the most imposing of all the surviving figures, rushes towards the right, her legs astride, in order to attack the Giant Enceladus, of whom only the bottom of the left leg is preserved. Further right, another half-fallen giant contorts his body abruptly forward. At the corners, a further two giants, apparently emerging from the earth, seem ready to launch into battle.

The Antenor Kore (no. 681). This monumental and majestic statue of a mature woman stood on the plinth nowadays exhibited alongside it (actually the upper section of its high base). The inscription on the plinth informs us that the statue was a votive offering of the potter Nearchos and a creation of the sculptor Antenor. A markedly tectonic work. *Circa* 500 BC.

Kore no. 1360. A tall, much damaged kore which, though incomplete and much deteriorated, is clearly one of the finest examples of the type. The precision and delicacy of its execution are particularly remarkable. Comparison with the Antenor kore clearly reveals that the difference between them is not of date, but of artistic conception. The work of the Athenian Antenor is of monumental aspect and its virtues are of a structural nature. Kore 1360 is distinguished by its finely worked surface and the gentle undulations of the drapery and hair. Most probably a Parian work. Late 6th century BC.

Statue of a Flying Nike (no. 691). This petite and joyous figure with widespread wings flies left. Clad in a chiton and himation, her luxuriant hair billows along her back. Possibly a Chian work. *Circa* 500 BC.

Kore with Dove (no. 683). This kore seems somewhat strange amidst the others. Her large head, short legs and long arms give the distinct impression of a dwarf. *Circa* 510 BC.

Giant from the centre
of the pediment with
the battle of Gods and
Giants.

Impetuous giant from
the right edge of the
same pediment as
7444.

The Antenor
Kore (c. 500 BC).

Small Archaic male
head, no. 621.
Circa 500 BC.

ALCOVE

Displayed in the alcove are minor objects, only some of which come from the Acropolis; the majority were found in excavations conducted by G. Miliadis to the south of the rock, in the Sanctuary of the Nymphs, between 1955 and 1958. Of the sculptures from the Acropolis excavations, special mention may be made of the following: The head of a kore no. 659, though badly damaged, is very sweet and fresh. It is probably an Ionian work of 520 - 510 BC. The small head of an athlete, in "Severe" style (*circa* 460 BC), the calves of a Cycladic kore of 500 - 490 BC, the head of a bearded man on which much of the coloration is preserved (500 BC.).

Exhibited in this small gallery are some of the most important works not only of the Acropolis Muse-

The "Blond *Boy*"
Circa 480 BC

Painting dating from 510-500 BC.

GALLERY VI

um, but of ancient Greek art as a whole, for they mark the most crucial period in its development, i.e. the transition from the Archaic phase to the Classical, known conventionally as the Severe style. The birth of this style coincides with the interlude between the two Persian invasions, in 490 and 480 BC, though its roots are to be sought in the works of the preceding period.

One of the most significant pieces is the so-called "Critius Youth" (no. 698), a statue of an ephebe victorious in the games. It was found in the "Persian level" (see Historical Outline), for which reason its innovations are of great importance for the history of art, since it is one of the developmentally later works from that stratum. The contrapostal stance, in which the weight of the body is placed on one foot, thus causing counter movements in the body, is entirely new. The Archaic smile has disappeared, giving way to an aspect of intellectual concentration. But it is not only the innovations which are important in this work, it is its superb artistic quality. Indeed, it is very likely that the artist was the sculptor Critius, mentor of Myron, since the treatment is very reminiscent of the Harmodios and Aristogeiton group (the later group of the Tyrannicides, known only from copies) known from the sources to have been a work of his. Shortly before 480 BC.

"Blond Boy" (no. 689). Another masterpiece of the same years, but by a different artist, who was more intent on conveying spiritual depth, almost verging on melancholy. The statue takes its name from the colour preserved on the hair when the head was first discovered. The turn and inclination of the head indicate a contrapostal stance. Perhaps the hip no. 6478 is from the same piece. *Circa* 480 BC.

"Pensive Athena" (no. 695). Votive relief of *circa* 460 BC representing Athena gazing thoughtfully at a stele. The work is difficult to interpret, for though not the product of an atelier, it is influenced by the great art of the age.

Nike (Victory) (no. 690). Fragments of the statue of a Nike of 490 - 480 BC, which was attached to a columnar base with a dedicatory inscription of the polemarch Callimachos, who fell at Marathon (490 BC). If the join is correct, Callimachos had expressed the wish to dedicate the work before the battle, but this was actually fulfilled posthumously, in his name.

Painting of a running athlete (no. 67) of 510 -500 BC, in red-figure technique but with brown used for the body. The inscription initially referred to Megacles "kalos" (the fair and noble one), but the name was subsequently half-erased and replaced with the name Glaukytes. Megacles was a member of the rich and powerful Alcmeonid family and was exiled in 486 BC. It seems that it was then that the name on the inscription was altered to that of someone else.

Euthydicos' kore (nos 686 and 609). This kore was also found in the "Persian level". Its lower part still stands on the capital of its columnar base, on which the name of the dedicator, Euthydicos, is incised, though not that of the artist, unfortunately. The work dates to 490 BC and displays the characteristics of the transition from Archaic art to the Severe style (rectangular face, thick eyelashes, transformation of the incipient smile into a look of self-confidence). A strong work, possibly from the Peloponnese.

Front part of a horse (no. 697). The loveliest horse known in Archaic art. Lively, light and lissome, the planes of its body ripple. *Circa* 490 BC.

Ephebe (no. 692). Tender modelling with a diffuse powdery finish over the entire surface. Since the statue follows the kouros schema, it was evidently sculpted before the major innovation of contrapostal pose. *Circa* 490 BC.

Athena (no. 140). She was supported by her spear in the right hand, while the left is brought onto her waist. The strict contrapostal stance and thick, heavy peplos are indicative of a date *circa* 480 BC.

Head of an ephebe (no. 699). Much later than the other works in this room, this head with its contemplative expression dates from the time of the Parthenon. It is the work of an accomplished artist in Phidias' circle. A victorious athlete is represented, as apparent from the fillet in his hair.

Relief of "Pensive
Athena".
Circa 460 BC.

Ex voto of Athena,
no. 140.
Circa 480 BC.

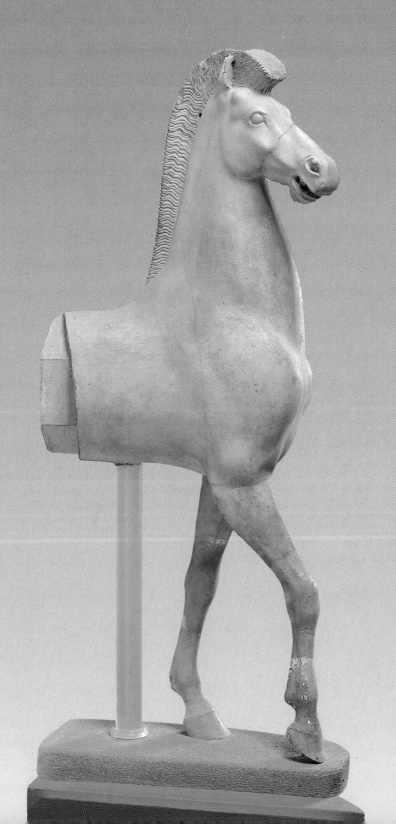

Front part
of a horse.
Circa 490 BC.

Torso of an ephebe.
Circa 490 BC.

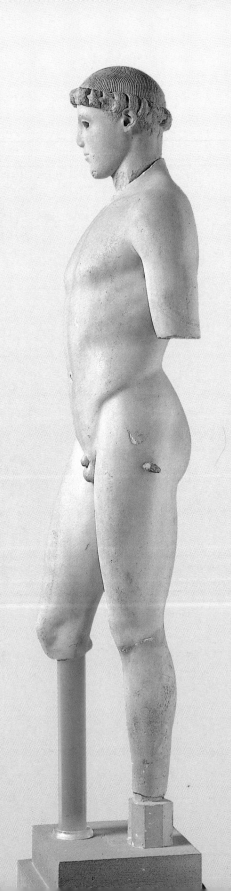

Kore dedicated by
Euthydicos.
Circa 490 BC.

Fragment of the
north frieze of the
Parthenon. Head of
a horse, no. 1130.

GALLERY VII

This gallery is devoted entirely to pieces from the sculpted decoration of the Parthenon.

We note first and foremost the sections of the colossal figures from the pediments of the temple. The magnificent athletic torso of Hephaestus (no. 880) and the spare yet firm one of Selene (no. 881) belong to the east pediment. Part of the taut, muscular body of Poseidon (only the chest section is original, the rest is a plaster copy of the original in the British Museum), the powerful yet fluidly modelled trunk of the kneeling Ilissos (no. 887), and fragments from horses' heads (nos 882, 884) are all from the west pediment.

Also on display is one of the metopes from the south side of the Parthenon, no. 705, showing a Centaur seizing a Lapith woman by the waist, a work of outstanding plasticity and convincing corporeal details.

Ranged around the walls are fragments of the Parthenon frieze, metopes and pediments. Fragments of the frieze which merit attention are: the head of Iris with her serious countenance (no. 855), the head of an ephebe beside that of a horse (nos 1134 - 1127), the lifelike head of a horse (no. 1130).

On the jamb of the doorway leading from gallery VI to gallery VII are the strikingly realistic heads of Centaurs (nos 727, 720). On the jambs of the doorway into gallery VIII are the head of a Lapith (no. 6511) from a metope, and that of a Lapith woman (no. 1309), likewise from a metope.

Metope from the south
face of the Parthenon,
no. 705.

Fragment of plaque
XXI from the south
frieze of the Parthenon,
no. 1134.

Fragment of plaque V
from the east frieze of
the Parthenon.
Head of Iris, no. 855.

Torso of Poseidon,
from the west pediment of
the Parthenon, no. 885.

GALLERY VIII

Plaques from the Parthenon frieze are exhibited on the south, east and part of the north wall of this gallery, in the same order as on the building. On the transverse wall projecting from the north are figures from the Erechtheum frieze. The remainder of the north wall and the entire west one are devoted to plaques from the parapet of the Nike temple.

Parthenon frieze: Of the plaques of the east frieze, we pause at no. 856 which depicts, seated in serene majesty, the deities Poseidon, Apollo and Artemis, and alongside them Aphrodite, of whom only the head and lower part of her garment have survived. This plaque is frequently attributed to the atelier of the sculptor Alcamenes. From the north frieze we single out plaque 857 with the ephebes driving bovines for sacrifice, a work of great ethos and sensitive rendering; plaque 864 with the pitcher-bearers, calm figures with penetrating gaze, plaque 865 with the bearers of olive branches, plaques 874, 871, 859 representing the dismounting contest (*apobates*), and plaques with youths on horseback 863, 861, 862. Of the plaques from the south frieze, on the north wall of the gallery, no. 868 merits attention.

Nike parapet: The decoration of the Nike parapet is sometimes dated *circa* 420 - 415 BC and sometimes after 410 BC. Certainly these works are among the loveliest of the so-called "rich" style which dominated post-Parthenon art, in the years of the Peloponnesian war. We note especially plaque 972, showing two Nikes dragging a reluctant bull calf to sacrifice, which was sculpted by two different artists; 977 with a Nike ascending the steps of the Nike tower, 989 with a seated Athena and a Nike (no. 974) before her, bedecking a now-lost trophy, and lastly, the famous plaque 973 where the Nike adjusts the sandle on her raised foot. In this last piece the accomplished rendering of the diaphanous garment, which clings to the body as if wet, is indeed remarkable.

Erechtheum frieze: The small figures of Pentelic marble were sculpted separately and subsequently accommodated on the relief surface of the ground of dark Eleusinian marble (which stone has been used as the background in this display). The theme is difficult to decipher. The figures were probably executed by stonecarvers, yet maintain the high artistic standards of the period. In the building inscription of the Erechtheum, of the year 409 BC, the names of some of the artisans engaged in modelling the figures of the frieze are mentioned.

Plaque VI from the east
frieze of the Parthenon,
no. 856.

Figure of Apollo,
detail of plaque VI.

Figure of Artemis,
detail of plaque VI.

Plaque XXIX from the
north frieze of the
Parthenon. Horsemen
no. 863.

Plaque XXXI from the
north frieze of the
Parthenon. Horsemen.
no. 862.

Plaque II from tl
north frieze of tl
Parthenon. Youtl
driving animals
sacrifice, no. 85

Plaque VI from the
north frieze of the
Parthenon, no. 864.

Plaque XVII from the
south frieze of the
Parthenon. Horsemen,
no. 868.

Plaque from the parapet of the
temple of Athena Nike.
Athena, seated left (no. 989),
receives an offering from the
Nike (no. 974) standing right.

Plaque from the
parapet of the
temple of Athena
Nike. Two Nikai
driving a bull to
sacrifice, no. 972.

Left section of a
plaque from the
parapet of the
temple of Athena
Nike. Nike
ascending steps,
no. 977.

Plaque from the
parapet of the temple of
Athena Nike. Seated
Athena, no. 981.

Plaque from the parapet of the temple of Athena Nike. Nike loosening her sandal, no. 973.

Figures from the
Erechtheum frieze,
no. 1073.

Figure of a Nike from
the Erechtheum frieze,
no. 2825.

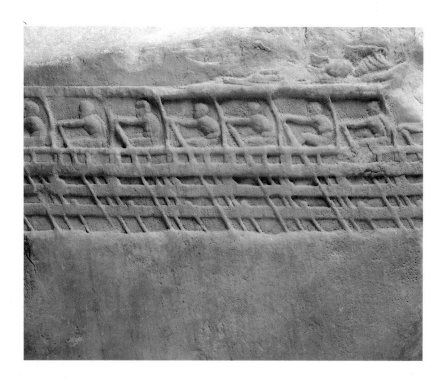

The "Lenorman"
relief. Late 5th century BC.

GALLERY IX

The exhibits in the final gallery of the Acropolis Museum were re-arranged just a few years ago. Most of the pieces previously on display were removed so that the original Korai from the Erechtheum could be housed there in a controlled environment, after their dismantling from the building, in order to protect them from erosion due to atmospheric pollution, and their replacement by copies. As has been said already, the Caryatids, six in number, supported the roof of the southwest porch in Π-shaped arrangement; four on the front, one on the west leg and one on the east.

Four of the Caryatids can be seen in the Acropolis Museum, since the second from the left on the front row is now in the British Museum, and only fragments of that which stood at the northeast corner have survived.

There are early precedents for the use of anthropomorphic supports in Greek architecture, particularly female figures (Siphnian Treasury at Delphi). The freshness and vitality of the Erechtheum Korai, works of the years 420 - 415 BC, transform the tectonic prop into a dynamic aesthetic axis of the edifice. They are the creations of a great artist of the school of Phidias (perhaps Alcamenes). The subtle play of pleats on the body, the harmonious flow of the dense folds on the weight-bearing limb and the flexion of the free one are truly wonderful.

Caryatid from the
Erechtheum.

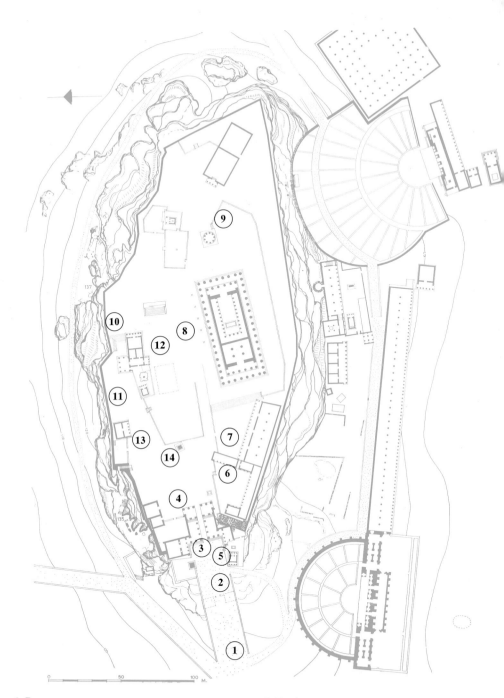

1. Ramp

2. Beulé Gate

3. Pedestal of the statue of Agrippa

4. Propylaea

5. Temple of Athena Nike

6. Sanctuary of Artemis Brauronia

7. Chalkotheke

8. Parthenon

9. Temple of Roma and Augustus

10. Erechtheum

11. Pandroseion

12. Ancient temple

13. House of the Arrephoroi

14. Statue of Athena Promachos